HOW TO COMMUNICATE WITH SPIRIT GUIDES

A Psychic Development Work book

Tasha Roubion

Dedicated to Mariah and Rachel. Without you two I would still be floundering in the wind.

FOREWORD

S pirit connected Tasha and me through the editing of this book and I couldn't be more grateful. I've found Tasha to be an esteemed psychic who is not only tuned into Spirit, but one who listens to and heeds the messages as well. Tasha has done several personal and business readings for me. I find her work to be accurate, thought-provoking, and enlightening.

Here's the coolest thing—I've been using the blind scenarios method to develop my connection with Spirit Guides. It's really true that anyone can do this! I was taught to believe that only certain or "special" people were gifted with intuition. That's not true. Everyone has the capability to connect and develop psychic gifts. Even better, the blind scenarios method is an excellent way to cultivate your intuition. The more I work with it, the easier it is for me to tune into the messages, make sense of them, and most importantly, trust them.

This book can help you do the same! Here's to your cherished connection with your Spirit Guides.

Tasha Roubion

Melissa Drake
Founder, Collaborative AF

WHO ARE SPIRIT GUIDES (AKA GUIDES)?

M uch like we have teachers and mentors here on earth, we also have them on the other side. Guides are our soul's teacher! They are with us through all of our trials and errors. They are loving, supporting, and not judgmental as you may think. Just like we have personalities on earth, our Guides have personalities as well. Some Guides are more serious, some are loving goofballs, but all of them share the common thread of wanting to connect with us on a deeper level. Above all, they are very patient with us. Most have been on this earth before as well, so they understand just how difficult life can be. They are our biggest cheerleaders.

Throughout each life, we usually have one main Guide with us from the moment we are born until the time we cross over. We also have other Guides who come in from time to time to help us with specific parts of our journey. Different Guides serve different purposes in our life. For this journey, let's imagine we are communicating with our main Guide for the time being. Over time, you may be able to differentiate between specific Guides as they enter your consciousness to work with you.

One thing that helped me build a close relationship with my Guide was learning her name. It is such a simple concept, but a seemingly difficult thing to learn. What worked best for me was asking my Guide to reveal her name through the world around me. After I asked for that insight, a single name began to jump out. I began hearing the same name on the radio, in songs, on the television, and in movies. Don't be surprised if it is a name you are already familiar with or have even named a pet! Your Guide's name is near and dear to your heart, even if you don't consciously remember it. Another method to learn a Guide's name is to simply ask them to reveal it. I've heard the first name that comes to mind is it. I'm stubborn and like proof, which is why I asked my Guide to divulge it to me instead. For those who are curious, my Guide's name is Laura!

> My understanding of Spirit Guides may be different
> from yours. It is *okay* to believe different things on this
> journey. The energy of what we do remains the same.

The purpose of this book and course workbook is to teach you to communicate with your Guides. There are many reasons establishing and cultivating this connection with your Guides is beneficial. You may want to communicate with Guides to help others, do psychic work, or to fine-tune your own intuition. Being aware of your own connection is a valuable tool for everyone. There is an amazing world of spiritual discovery, available for those who wish to connect. While this work involves effort and determination, it's not difficult and the benefits are worth it.

CONGRATULATIONS ON CHOOSING THIS JOURNEY OF CONNECTION!

T he most common question clients ask me is, "How do I talk to my Guides?" I was inspired to create this book to empower clients to facilitate their own connection with their Guides. I tell everyone, "You can do this too!" Now, I'll help you do just that.

We are all created with a divine connection to the other side. In this way, a piece of us remains, energetically, forever connected to our home away from Earth. We are able to communicate and do psychic work by connecting to our higher self and our Spirit Guides. Everyone can develop connection if they have the desire to do so.

When you research the topic of communicating with your Spirit Guides, it is easy to become overwhelmed by the information you find. I've read you must meditate for four hours a day, you must be vegan, and you must be completely healed by doing "shadow work" before even beginning. Here's the great news: It's not that complicated! Plus, I'm here to guide you through the process.

Every single person has different needs and soul goals. Our differences create unique understandings of how this world works. I believe there is usually truth in everything we believe. As such, this book does not highlight specific philosophies. Instead, it focuses on how to actually do the work of connecting to Guides and receiving the guidance they offer. To sum it up - If you want to communicate with your Guides, you can. All you need is an open heart, an open mind, and the willingness to look a little silly from time to time. That's part of the process! I encourage you to embrace your own unique abilities, have fun, and enjoy learning to communicate with your own Guides.

WHAT NOT TO DO

Sometimes finding the best path involves taking some wrong turns! When I began, I tried the main methods given to budding psychics. I tried guessing the colors someone was thinking of. I tried to psychically see what someone was holding in their hands. I tried to intuitively determine the number of beans in a jar. Nothing worked! According to these rudimental tests, I was not psychic. It was discouraging to say the least. Even if I got something right once in a while, there was no consistency in the accuracy. There was no valid proof that my abilities were real, that the efforts worked, or that I was even connecting to this super power. I questioned how I could ever give a reading to someone and feel confident the answers I gave were accurate. Everyone needs validation — even psychics.

I have come to understand, our Guides communicate with us so we can help others. When the guidance doesn't come in the way we expect, many give up. Now I know different. Guides do not communicate with us for our ego's sake. They don't communicate with us so we can run and tell everyone we are psychic and wear "I Am Psychic" T-shirts we found on Amazon. The methods listed above do not help anyone. Therefore, Guides generally don't have time to play those games with us. In other words, they don't entertain ego.

The reason I'm sharing what did not work for me is to offer personal encouragement to keep going. All you need to do psychic work is have a true desire to be of assistance to others or create growth in your own life.

There has only been one method of connection that provides consistent results for me. It is a method created with two dear friends as we explored the world around us and what it means to be a true psychic. We call it the "Scenarios Method."

THE SCENARIOS METHOD

W hen you first try to communicate with your Guide, you should consider your purpose for connecting. People who connect for personal growth or to help others will see huge improvements in a short period of time. When Guides know our hearts, they get excited to teach us their language! When we take the energy of helping others and merge it with the practice of tapping into this gift, we can be consistent in our accuracy. Through this consistency, we receive the validation we need to trust the messages we receive from Spirit.

The practice begins with thoughts of a hypothetical situation a person may need your help with. We call these hypothetical situations, "Scenarios." What is a scenario? To put it simply, a scenario is a fake problem a fake person has.

Here is a sample of a scenario: "A client approaches you because they are struggling to find their purpose." When you try to receive the message for your hypothetical client, all you do is close your eyes and connect. Merriam-Webster defines connect as, "bring together or into contact so that a real or notional link is established." This connection enables you to link with your Spirit Guide. There is no mysterious trick to connecting to your Guide. You use your imagination, and you're tapped in. What you see, hear, feel, and experience is all part of the connection to your Guide. Once you close your eyes to connect, write down everything. No detail is too small. Once you have done this, you will begin to peel back the layers to how your Guide communicates with you. You'll discover symbols for relationships, careers, finances, fears, and hopes. You'll learn to feel the emotions associated with the messages. You'll learn to read between the lines of what you used to believe were just daydreams.

The most important aspect of this teaching method is not to know what the scenario is before you connect and tap in. You connect to the energy *blindly.* This means you've got no idea what's going on. Doing this, you learn you are able to receive actual messages that pertain to the situation without even knowing what the situation is. This is the best proof that your connection is genuine. Further, it strengthens your own awareness to what you're capable of, while developing trust between you and your Guide. Once you learn you do not even need to know the scenario to deliver an accurate message, nothing will hold you back.

The beauty of this blind scenario method is you are learning to trust the connection you have with your Guides. When the day comes that someone asks you a question that is straight to the point, you will not struggle near as much to interpret what their Guide is trying to say. This method forces you to analyze the results you get first, learn the language second, and trust in the connection third. Providing an answer to a friend or client is much easier when you know the question beforehand. This is a trust building exercise.

When you first begin, you need to understand everything will not make sense to you right away. It is through repetition and practice that you recognize what each symbol stands for. You may see a balloon rising in the sky for an upcoming birthday celebration. You may see a person standing at a cross-roads when they're facing a difficult choice. Each vision is unique and represents a different message based on the images you see and the way you feel when you see them. With experience and practice, you will begin to intuitively understand what your Guide is saying to you.

If you get stuck with your interpretation, and simply have no clue what they're trying to say, you can google dream symbols and their interpretation for further clarification. I do this all the time! People have studied symbols for a long time, and Spirit will use all the tools available at our disposal to clue us in. Dream interpretation websites are invaluable to develop psychic abilities. For instance, if your client is avoiding a challenging situation in their life, you may see a bumble bee. One of the interpretations on dream-meaning.net reveals, "Dreaming of bees means you are trying to avoid a negative or painful situation."

The quickest way to develop this gift or skill is to work with a partner. When you are with a partner, you can steer each other through the visions. A partner can see from an objective point of view and discern, where you need to focus your attention in the vision. After practicing for a while, this will become more natural, and you will begin to intuitively know what aspects of the vision are demanding your attention and how to look for details.

Your creative mind is not limited in how you seek and receive the information from your Guides. You control these visions just as much as your Guides direct them. The communication and messages conveyed truly are a team effort. Our Guides work with us and where we're at in our visions.

Some notes to consider: You are able to fast-forward or rewind time in visions. You can walk within your vision and move in any direction. You can ask your Guide to simply show you what the issue is. If you see a home, you can enter it. If you feel lost, you can consider this may be something the person you're reading for is experiencing. All of these thoughts, feelings, and findings are valuable pieces of the puzzle.

Each person and their Guide will have a unique way of communicating with one another. Our Guides use information already deeply ingrained in us to get a message across to others. When I get visions, I see a lot of nature and wildlife. When my developing partner gets visions, she often sees car parts or tools. She understands how they work and what they represent. Our Guides will instinctively choose things that resonate with us on a personal level.

The Scenarios Method works on all psychic senses. When we tap in, we get visions to develop clairvoyance, or clear seeing. We listen to develop clairaudience, or clear hearing. We feel emotions to develop clairsentience, or clear sensing. These all develop naturally as you practice. There are no limitations with the Scenario Method. You can grow infinitely the more you are committed to the practice. You may find your abilities shift over time. One week you may have visions that are out of this world, and the next week hear things better. Your body may be covered in goosebumps, or you may feel sick to your stomach when receiving messages. We have subtle shifts as we grow into our gifts, but we are *always* growing. The Scenarios Method helps build all of your senses at one time. Remember not to get frustrated if you see amazing sights one day and struggle for connection with visions the next day. Psychics are still human! Growing your psychic gifts is similar to strength training. We have periods of having less energy and periods of having more energy. The longer you practice though, the more stamina, energy, and consistency your psychic muscle holds.

When I do a reading for a client, I set my intention to connect to their Guide instead of my own. Spirit Guides are willing to work with psychics and mediums to deliver messages. Things are known in advance on the other side and I've never had a Spirit Guide show up late!

Connecting with Guides for others is a valuable learning experience for everyone involved. The client or friend can receive help with making decisions, they can learn more about their relationships, or clarify certain aspects of their life that they are having trouble navigating. One thing to note, is Spirit Guides very rarely tell someone what they *must* do. We all have free will and Spirit does not take that away from us. We can ask for their opinion from time to time, and they are usually happy to assist us on this journey.

When you first begin reading for others, it's important to share everything you receive. In my readings, I found that other people's Guides share important validations through the visions I receive. Because of this fact, I always share everything. A recent reading showed a client wearing white tennis shoes with a black stripe on them. I shared that information with her and she said she has a pair of Adidas tennis shoes that she wears daily. If you don't know, the Adidas brand has black stripes they are renowned for. This image was confirmation for the client that I was connected on a psychic level. It is often those tiny details that speak to clients the loudest. When I see clients sitting in their pajamas, eating a particular brand of cereal, I share. Any emotions I feel during the reading, I share. Any funny word, quirky or silly image I see or think, I share it. Spirit has a great sense of humor.

After you grow in experience and know without a doubt the message your Guide or their Guide is wishing to share with someone, you may not feel it necessary to share *all* the details of the vision. It is a personal decision for all of us. Some psychics tell the basics. That works fine for them. As long as they are accurate, their clients are happy. I'm personally a chatter box and like to share every nuance of the reading.

Very often, a client will have an alternate interpretation of a message you give when you share the entire vision. They may intuitively understand their Guide's symbolism more than you in certain cases. Their understanding does not invalidate the message you give to them, it simply expands the message and leads to more clarity. One vision can have many, many layers of meanings. I welcome additional interpretations. To me, it's as if their Guides are playing Spirit charades with us. Through these interpretations, we work as a team to interpret messages. I feel, the reason psychics will not ever be 100% accurate is because we use our human minds to interpret the spiritual information we receive. It is our job to learn the symbols our Guides use, to the best of our ability, so we may become adept at understanding the messages we are receiving. This can help you in many ways: you can give trustworthy messages to clients, have better relationships in your own life, grow spiritually, and learn to trust your intuition.

Some people believe you need a picture of the person to read for them. Some believe you need to be in person. Some believe you need their birthday, address, or ZIP Code. These are just some examples of the many personal beliefs that exist in the spiritual community. I'm here to tell you, whatever your beliefs are, is how it's going to work for you. I do most of my readings long-distance and without a picture. I've never had any difficulties connecting to a person's Guide. In my experience, I've found, the only limitations we have, are the limitations we place on ourselves.

With this workbook, you will be working independently on the Scenarios Method. This is an invaluable way to practice and develop. If you can, find a partner or best friend to work with you too. While it's not required, it does make the experience of working with your Spirit Guides even more fun and exciting. I have also found, it is easier to interpret the messages when you have two minds working collectively. You will have to be diligent in researching the symbols at first if you do not intuitively under-stand what your Guides are saying. Every single aspect of any in-formation you receive, is valid in one way or another. It is your job to connect the dots. If you tap in and see the color red, you have to learn and understand why your Guide showed that color to you. It is your job to investigate what the color red represents in relation to the scenario you're considering. Draw as many con-nections as you can and you will find that you can deliver a more rich and detailed reading to prospective clients and friends.

TAPPING IN TO RECEIVE MESSAGES

T apping in is creating a connection between you and your Guide. It is very simple to do. You ask to connect, close your eyes, and begin. When I first began, I assumed it would feel like visions were pouring into my head. I would look around, disappointed, that I was only seeing black. The visions do come on strong sometimes, but most of the time we start by creating the vision ourselves. You may have a particular setting you want to start the vision at. You may want to picture your client sitting in their home. You have the power to create the time and setting to receive information. Our Guides will work with the setting we create to pass us the necessary information. When I first began, I always imagined myself in a field of grass to start. Now, I never know where I'm going to be when I close my eyes. The longer you do this work, the quicker the visions come on.

When you close your eyes, you may experience seeing gray shapes, gray outlines, weird symbols, or letters floating in the air.

My developing partner and I call this space Spirit Symbols Land. We don't like Spirit Symbols Land because it is difficult to get any real messages from that place. We often encounter this place when our minds are restless or our outside world is too chaotic. Meditation can help quiet your mind if you find yourself in Spirit Symbols Land too often. What you need to do if you enter that space, is relax your body, and go deeper into your mind. For me, going deeper feels like sliding down and back into my brain. The space in your mind to get to the true messages feels like it's in the place that stores and creates memories. It's also in the area of the mind we use to daydream or fantasize.

When you relax and slide back into the vision, take in every detail you can. If you are in a forest, what level is the light? Are the trees thin or thick? What season is it? Is there water? What do you hear? What does it feel like there? What is the temperature? Is there any precipitation? Is there wind blowing? Are you feeling calm, nervous, anxious, excited, or hopeful?

Sometimes, we get "stuck" when we tap in. We sit there and nothing changes within our vision. We look around, waiting for something to happen, and it just doesn't. When this occurs, it is your responsibility to interact with the vision you are having. Begin psychically walking within the world you and your Guides have created. What do you come across? Which direction did you begin walking? For me personally, the left of my vision is the past and movement to the right of my vision represents the future. You can tell your Guide you'd like use the same left/right method if you'd like. You may see an animal or person in the vision who can direct you. You may end up following a rabbit down a trail. Again, I want to repeat, you are only limited by your own creativity with this development. You are not powerless in the settings for visions, symbols and interpretations.

You can ask your Guide to get specific. It's okay to state, "Show me what the issue is," to see changes within the vision. Sure, sometimes a client comes to you who is having an amazing time in their life and they want a big thumbs up. It does happen! But most of the time, people come to psychics because there are issues they need help resolving in their life. It is our job to pass their Guide's message to them in a way they can understand.

You may feel like you are making the vision up. That's normal. You may feel foolish and silly. That is normal too. Don't shy away from being vulnerable in this process though, because there is so much to gain from developing your connection and psychic senses.

There are usually two main parts to a psychic reading that you need to identify the most. There is the energy of the situation the client is going through, and the energy of the message the Guide is trying to give. When you first begin, you may only get one or the other. Over time, it's important to seek both. If you feel a vision coming to a close, it is good practice to ask the Guide, "What is the overall message?"

On rare occasions, I will meet someone who can not see visions. If this is you, there is hope. One of my development partners started out the same way. With continued practice, it's possible to get the hang of it. An exercise to build the third eye, known as the inner eye, is to close your eyes and picture something you are already familiar with. Draw the object or situation out in your mind. Hold on to the image for as long as you can. Psychically walk around this object and change the lighting if you can. Consider the tree in your yard, a pet you have, a loved one. Make yourself see them in your mind's eye and fill in as many details as you can. Doing this repeatedly will strengthen your third eye abilities. You can still practice the scenarios using other senses to support and enhance the connection to your Guides.

When you feel emotions as you're tapping in, lean into this emotion. If you experience sadness, ask your Guides more questions such as: "Where does this emotion stem from?" or "What is the root cause of this emotion?" Those emotions are tools for you to explore. When you see objects, explore them. If you see a home, go inside. Look at the interior of the house. What pictures do the walls hold? Be curious and bold with your exploration of spiritual communication.

Every time you ask a question to your Guide while you are tapped in, it is like turning the key to greater understanding.

You should know, this work takes a ton of mental and emotional energy! You may find you can only do one or two scenarios at a time before you feel energetically depleted and physically tired. You may see a fluctuation in your accuracy levels if you push yourself too hard. You can become physically exhausted from this work if you push beyond your limits. Psychic gifts are like a muscle and it takes practice to build up stamina. Do not burn yourself out. Take your energy levels very seriously. They are an indication of progress and remind you to take care of yourself. One key way to care for yourself while doing this work is to drink extra water.

One final note! Guides may use your personal life as you're tapping in to the scenarios listed. Don't be surprised if you get personal messages about yourself or loved ones when you review the work you've done.

EXAMPLES OF THE VISIONS
I EXPERIENCED

W ith this first example, I want to share how abstract these visions are sometimes. I want to show you how we may not always understand immediately what is going on, but it is still important to trust the information received is always a valid message.

A client came to me wanting general messages from her Guides. She had some topics in mind, but she wanted to see what her Guide said first.

At the beginning of the vision, I saw my client adjusting a necktie around a man's head. What was so crazy about this vision, is this head was just floating in mid-air! After she adjusted the neck-tie, she carried it with her to a classroom. She appeared unhappy and had a scowl on her face. She sat down, put the head on the desk beside her, and began to take notes. She looked deflated and was writing "XOXO" on her paper. She was also raising her hand and answering questions. This was a pretty wild vision, even for me!

I interpreted the vision to mean she was trying to help someone make adjustments in their life but she was unhappy with the results. As she was in a class with this head, I understood there was more learning to do about the situation. I understood her Guides were encouraging her to participate in her own life. I also understood she needed to be active and willing to learn more about the situation that was bothering her. I felt pretty good about the interpretation considering how odd the vision was!

With permission, I am sharing her exact response. "My husband has high-functioning Asperger's and has been extremely moody our entire relationship. It has escalated severely over the last six to seven months. In fact, just a few days ago, he was ready for a divorce. That's when he apologized for what he calls 'periodically getting upset and losing his mind' He doesn't realize what he's saying or how he's acting is so terrible. We're going to be starting a new marriage therapist. This has been extremely stressful for me."

As soon as I saw her note that he describes those periods as "losing his mind" I immediately understood the floating head. It was Spirit's symbol for losing one's mind or losing one's head. Spirit really does have a sense of humor to lighten the mood sometimes.

Her being in the class with her husband's head was reflecting going to the marriage counselor with him. Even though she looked sad during the process, she continued to raise her hand and participate. The XOXO's I saw her write reflected the class she was in dealt with her romantic relationship.

I'm sharing this reading first because it is important to understand that we may not always know the entire point. We are the messengers. It is our job to interpret the best we can, but Spirit is speaking through us.

In the second scenario, I want to highlight how our Guides send validations to their person that they are watching over them. With this reading, a woman simply wanted a message about her relationship. No other information was shared. In the vision, I saw the woman sitting on a couch. Her husband rested his head on her lap, looking up at her. As I watched them, his eyes turned into galaxies and he began to dissolve in mid-air. I explained I felt this was symbolic for her feeling the "cosmic connection" was fading. She validated that was true. She also told me that only three days earlier, she told her husband his eyes reminded her of galaxies.

Not every psychic shares the symbolic visions they receive. Some psychics simply share the messages they are receiving. I have personally found that the smallest details woven throughout the symbolic visions are equally as important to share. How you deliver messages is entirely up to you!

I have been shown what a person ate earlier in the day. I have been shown an action they were doing immediately before receiving the reading. These small details create the feeling of being seen and guided. It shows that we are watched over, loved and protected, even in the most mundane moments of our life. The most astounding readings aren't always the ones that reveal a person's soul purpose. They are often just readings that give validation after validation that small parts of our life are noticed. As Oprah states, a human's greatest desire is to be seen. These small but significant messages let clients know they are seen and their Guides pay attention to details.

In another reading, I had a very delicate topic come up. A woman wanted to know why her beautiful young niece had to pass away so soon. Her niece was only six months old. I was doing a tarot reading for her, but I also wanted to tap in psychically or with mediumship abilities first.

When I connected with her, I saw a rainbow forming and then two hands posed in prayer. I shared that information with the client. The lady got back to me and told me her niece's name had meant, "Heavenly Rainbow."

In my visions, I have found that waters are usually emotions. If the waters are calm and serene, the client's emotions are normally peaceful. If I'm looking at a stormy ocean, with waves tossing about wildly, the client is usually feeling out of control. If I see someone walking through the desert, I understand their emotions are not fulfilled or their needs are not being met. I've seen people holding a backpack when they are preparing for a journey. When I see someone tightening their shoelaces, I understand they are getting prepared for movement in their life. These are some examples of what I personally see. For you, the symbols and meanings may be wildly different. This is highly personal and unique work. While connection is most definitely not a science, the energy can be the same. Through a disciplined approach, you can learn to understand powerful messages in a consistent and reliable way.

TRUST THE PROCESS!

As you're learning to connect, be kind to yourself. Do not beat yourself up if you feel something did not work or immediately resonate. Negative emotions are blocks to our abilities. Also, there could be a reason why certain things don't work out the way you expect them to. Not all information is meant to be shared. Some Guides want their student to figure out a specific topic on their own. Sometimes you simply needed to go further with a vision and stopped too soon. A large part of developing your intuition involves trust and an ability to continue — especially when the current messages don't make sense. It requires perseverance and loyalty to continue even if you don't receive the instant gratification of complete understanding. The messages may or may not make sense over time. Either way, it's good that you're developing.

THE ETHICS OF GIVING
PSYCHIC READINGS

One thing I want to speak about briefly before you begin developing, is the ethics of this type of work. People who go to psychics often place a high value on what the psychic says. They're eager to hear advice, future predictions, or things that should be avoided in their life. Your words carry weight. **You should not ever do a reading or share details that elicits fear in another human being.** If you cause someone fear, then you are misunderstanding the message their Guide is trying to give or you were not sensitive in the delivery of the information you received.

They say love is blind, fear is blind as well. Our Guides and spiritual helpers do not give information to scare us. As a human, we can misinterpret the information we receive. I have thought many, many times that someone I loved was going to die. I saw a sign! I had a dream! We are human, we fear. In tarot, the death card symbolizes endings and new beginnings. Death in tarot represents releasing your fears to embrace a new journey ahead of you. As death is so universal and symbolic — you may see it from time to time in your visions! It has not ever (in my experience) been literal. In fact, my Guides know I don't wish to see physical death for a client.

My ethics are I will not ever tell someone when a person is going to die even if those details are available to me. That is my personal hard and fast rule. Even if someone was going to die, the Guide giving messages would more than likely encourage your client to spend more time with their loved ones. They would encourage them to cherish their loved ones. We don't have to point-blank say "Uncle Frank is going to die on Tuesday," for them to get the message that they need to hear.

As with any profession, people who claim they are psychics have a wide range of personalities and ethics. Some psychics say they will banish an evil attachment from you for an additional $200. In my opinion, that is an example or poor ethics. It even causes me to question the legitimacy of their development.

As you are on this journey, look deep within yourself to help you determine where you stand on the moral fences that this work requires. Understand that you are fallible and human in this experience. If you are unsure of how to share a certain type of message, ask yourself how you would like to receive it.

Always be honest, but with a careful and concerting nature. Use your words wisely. On this journey, they hold a lot of power.

BEFORE YOU BEGIN — REMEMBER THIS:

1. You can create the setting to begin a vision. Simply picture a place in your mind.
2. You are never truly stuck because you can always create movement within the vision.
3. Ask to be shown the "issue" if nothing stands out to you.
4. Don't assume a vision is over just because you only receive two pieces of information. You can always go back for more.
5. You are a detective! You are a psychic detective and it is your job to investigate, to the best of your ability, what a Guide may be saying to you.
6. Avoid Spirit Symbols Land with the gray shadow figures. Relax into your mind and go *deeper*.
7. Google dream symbols for images you wrote down from your vision. Examples of dream symbols are specific types of insects, colors, animals, or objects.
8. Remember you are learning the language of your Spirit Guides. It would be insulting to believe what they share with you is unimportant or wrong. Be diligent in connect-

ing the dots. They are there.

9. There are usually at least two main sections of information to receive. First, there's the issues or scenario, and second, there's the message the Guide is trying to relay. One is dependent on the other for understanding, but they are independently important.

10. Don't take yourself too seriously when you begin developing your gift. This work is fun! Relax and adopt the energy of the child who is playing. Connect with joy and laughter. If you have a partner, ask goofy questions sometimes!

11. The only way to build trust in your authentic ability to connect is by starting each reading "blind." No peeking at the example scenario before tapping in.

12. Tapping in does not typically produce literal information. What you see will be symbolic to the energy of the scenario and the energy of the message.

13. While tapping in, when you experience an emotion, lean in to that emotion. Ask your Guide, "What is the root cause of this emotion?" or "Where does this emotion stem from?"

14. Every time you ask a question to your Guide, it is like turning a key into the door of greater understanding.

PRACTICING THE SCENARIO METHOD

Y ou will need a journal or computer to write down what you receive. This is going to be extremely important for you as you will keep track of your progress and all you learn. As you continue, these details will make up your spirit dictionary. It may evolve over time, but you will be pleased to see your connection grow stronger.

Your Guide is going to be excited to jump in to this work with you. You don't need any special equipment, just your creative mind, your openness, and your willingness to learn.

On each page, there will be a scenario created. It will be an issue that a prospective client or friend may need your help with or a message Spirit is trying to send.

Before you go to the next page to see the scenario, you need to tap in and write your notes if you are writing in a separate notebook. If you have purchased the paperback option, cover the top portion of the next page with a piece of paper so you don't see the scenario when you turn the page.

Here is an example of what your notebook could look like:
The vision I receive: (thoughts, emotions, symbols)
What is the issue:
What is the message:

Once you have recorded the details, you can turn the page and reveal the scenario. It is now up to you to put the pieces of the puzzle together. If you struggle with a certain ability, don't stress out about it. Work at your own pace and develop the areas you wish, when you wish to. For the first six months of my development, I only worked on seeing visions. If you don't understand the information at first, that's okay as well. Keep up with your progress, continue to practice and carefully consider the information you receive. The more you tap in, the more you will understand what you're receiving.

Helpful Hint: If you do all of the practice scenarios and wish to go again, simply select a page at random to practice again. You will always receive additional information and insights to scenarios you have worked on before.

I encourage everyone to develop the spark to divinity within. It is my desire to spread the light to as many people as possible. Our ability to connect has been kept silent for too long, and I wish to share my knowledge with all who are interested in discovering their own magic. I wish you abundance, love, and the joy of developing.

PART 2 - PSYCHIC WORKBOOK

The next section of the book contains the scenarios. You should have your pen and paper out if you are ready to begin. When you turn the page the first scenario will be visible. Go ahead and tap in now. Begin writing all you receive.

SCENARIO 1:

◆ ◆ ◆

Woman is unable to move forward from past love. She feels stuck in her life. She's not open to new relationships. She's harming herself by not being able to release the past.

SCENARIO 2:

◆ ◆ ◆

Person feels stuck in a toxic relationship. They have children with this person and are afraid to leave.

SCENARIO 3:

◆ ◆ ◆

Person is growing spiritually and feels an awakening within them. On some level they are afraid to leave behind what they are familiar with. Their Guides are encouraging them to embrace the journey.

SCENARIO 4:

◆ ◆ ◆

A new opportunity is coming soon for this person. Now is the time for them to plan their future and trust in the universe.

SCENARIO 5:

◆ ◆ ◆

Person is struggling right now with their thoughts and their emotions. They are creating scenarios that don't exist and are making themselves more paranoid than they need to be. They are focusing on the negative and embellishing it. Spirit is recommending that they find ways to center their thoughts, mind, and energy. They're encouraging them to focus on finding their inner peace.

SCENARIO 6:

◆ ◆ ◆

Client has been partying too much lately. They're being reckless with substances and they're focusing on the wrong priorities at this time. They need balance and moderation in their life. They need to find happiness in sobriety.

SCENARIO 7:

◆ ◆ ◆

Person is gay and struggling to accept it or come out of the closet. They're afraid of what other's will think.

SCENARIO 8:

◆ ◆ ◆

In this scenario, their Guides simply want to tell them they are doing a great job. They are proud of them and feel they've accomplished a lot.

SCENARIO 9:

◆ ◆ ◆

Someone needs a fresh start! They're clinging to old ideas or beliefs and those things are holding them back. They're encouraged to find new opportunities, to seek their passions and dreams. They're encouraged to do some deep soul searching to move past self-limiting beliefs.

SCENARIO 10:

◆ ◆ ◆

Spirit wishes to tell their student a new love is on the horizon. They're encouraged to keep their eyes and ears open to all of the signs around them.

`

SCENARIO 11:

◆ ◆ ◆

Client has an important test coming soon. Spirit is urging them to be diligent and put their best foot forward. Work hard!

SCENARIO 12:

◆ ◆ ◆

Person is struggling financially. They feel none of their hard work has paid off. What would their Guide's advice to them be?

SCENARIO 13:

◆ ◆ ◆

Person is overly superstitious and fearful. This is causing them to live in fear and unnecessary anxiety.

SCENARIO 14:

◆ ◆ ◆

Spirit is advising their student to seek additional counseling. They would benefit from a mental health professional.

SCENARIO 15:

◆ ◆ ◆

Person is being encouraged to see a doctor. They have physical issues that are important to resolve. If they wait too long, they could suffer serious consequences.

SCENARIO 16:

◆ ◆ ◆

Client's husband is away for work a lot. Client suspects infidelity. Husband is *not* cheating.

SCENARIO 17:

◆ ◆ ◆

Client has a history of abuse as a child. Spirit is recommending they seek counseling to help them cope with the trauma. Spirit is offering them love and words of encouragement.

SCENARIO 18:

◆ ◆ ◆

Client is struggling with communication in their life. They find it difficult to voice their true thoughts and hold themselves back from verbally expressing themselves.

SCENARIO 19:

◆ ◆ ◆

Client will have the opportunity to have a new pet in the near future! This pet could be a wonderful addition to their life.

SCENARIO 20:

◆ ◆ ◆

Client is facing consequences for actions they made in the past. Legal judgement is on the horizon for them.

SCENARIO 21:

◆ ◆ ◆

Client is at the very beginning of their spiritual journey. They are being encouraged to consider their life purpose at this time. Spirit is encouraging them to nurture themselves right now.

SCENARIO 22:

◆ ◆ ◆

Client's relationship in love is full of blessings, joy, and satisfaction. They are with a true soul partner and should embrace the one they're with. Spirit is encouraging gratitude.

SCENARIO 23:

◆ ◆ ◆

Spirit is encouraging this person to tap into their creative abilities right now. They should use their natural talents to bring beauty into the world around them.

SCENARIO 24:

◆ ◆ ◆

Client is focused too much on the material world around them. They are only concerned about wealth and status. They will never find true happiness with this mindset.

SCENARIO 25:

◆ ◆ ◆

Client will soon find themselves at a major crossroads in their life. They will be unsure of which path to take. They will be faced with many decisions.

SCENARIO 26:

◆ ◆ ◆

Client is going to be rewarded for all of their past efforts. A celebration is coming in the near future for them.

SCENARIO 27:

◆ ◆ ◆

Client's husband has a gambling addiction that is draining their resources.

SCENARIO 28:

◆ ◆ ◆

Client is battling suicidal tendencies. How would your Guides show you this?

SCENARIO 29:

◆ ◆ ◆

Client's old boyfriend has come back into the picture. He is trying to convince her to leave her marriage. Client is torn.

SCENARIO 30:

◆ ◆ ◆

Client has had an abortion in the past and feels intense guilt. They feel shame and remorse. What would their Guide's message to them be?

SCENARIO 31:

◆ ◆ ◆

Client has agoraphobia and is afraid to leave their house. They have become a hermit.

SCENARIO 32:

◆ ◆ ◆

Client is unhappy with their body weight. They are being encouraged to do physical exercise and work on their diet!

SCENARIO 33:

◆ ◆ ◆

Client wants a baby more than anything in the world. They are struggling with getting pregnant. Spirit wishes to tell them they *will* have a child.

SCENARIO 34:

◆ ◆ ◆

Client's family is religious and views their personal interests and views as dangerous.

SCENARIO 35:

◆ ◆ ◆

Client grew up without a father figure in their life. This has caused them to form unhealthy relationships with men.

SCENARIO 36:

◆ ◆ ◆

Client is being bullied by their co-workers. Spirit is encouraging them to stand up for themselves.

SCENARIO 37:

◆ ◆ ◆

Client feels they are repelling potential love interests. They are finding it difficult to find a partner. Client is encouraged to work on themselves first.

SCENARIO 38:

◆ ◆ ◆

Client is struggling to form bonds with their child. They didn't receive genuine love as a child and this has stunted their growth.

SCENARIO 39:

◆ ◆ ◆

Client has a social media addiction. It is causing them to view their own life unfairly. It is causing a strain in their relationships.

SCENARIO 40:

◆ ◆ ◆

Client is suffering from extreme burnout and exhaustion. They are being encouraged to rest and nurture themselves completely.

SCENARIO 41:

◆ ◆ ◆

Client is losing passion and connection with their spouse. They feel they have grown apart and are unsure of what to do.

SCENARIO 42:

◆ ◆ ◆

Client is feeling guilt over their sexual past. What would Spirit's message to them be?

SCENARIO 43:

◆ ◆ ◆

Jealousy is ruining your client's life. They are comparing themselves to everyone and they're seeing threats to their relationship when there are none.

SCENARIO 44:

◆ ◆ ◆

Client is happier than they have been in a long time. A season of abundance is upon them. Spirit is wishing them well.

SCENARIO 45:

◆ ◆ ◆

Client's Spirit Guide wishes to tell them that they are around. They wish to tell them they are watched over, seen, heard, and loved.

—

SCENARIO 46:

◆ ◆ ◆

Client's little sister has been stealing items from them. They are suspicious of this and have come to you for confirmation.

SCENARIO 47:

◆ ◆ ◆

Client has a child who is non-verbal. They are stressed but doing the best they can as a parent.

SCENARIO 48:

◆ ◆ ◆

Client has a dog that will be dying soon. Their pet is old and sick. Client is aware of this and wishes to know if their dog will be okay when they die.

SCENARIO 49:

◆ ◆ ◆

Client is being encouraged to bring more fun into their life. They are taking life too seriously. Spirit is saying life is meant to be enjoyed!

SCENARIO 50:

◆ ◆ ◆

Client is wishing to develop psychically. Spirit is saying they can do it.

ACKNOWLEDGEMENTS

I want to thank my beloved Spirit Guide, Laura. She has made her presence known in my life in so many magical ways. I am only consciously aware of her mentally and psychically, but my soul has known her forever. Thank you for being my Guide in this lifetime!

I want to acknowledge Mariah Carrico as the best friend and psychic development partner a girl could ever have. I'm so lucky to have found someone who is the exact same "style" of crazy as I am. How many people can you ask, "Do you want to be psychic?" And then get the response back of, "I SURE DO!!!" We are an amazing team. I truly believe we were meant to discover this psychic and spiritual world together. Soul sisters for eternity!

I want to acknowledge the best damn editor a person could wish for. Melissa Drake of collaborativeaf.com, you spoke straight to my heart with your red-pen editing process. You made my voice shine and made sure I used all of the proper commas and learned to tuck my period inside of the quotation mark! I'm so fortunate to work with someone who understood immediately what I was trying to say. You did not call me crazy! Thank you for working with me.

Lastly, I want to acknowledge my kids: Drake, Jackson, and Clara. Because they'll want to be included and I love you three bunches.

ABOUT THE AUTHOR

Tasha Roubion is a professional psychic who works predomin-
ately with Spirit Guide communication. She has delivered thou-
sands of readings to clients from all over the world. She offers
one-on-one mentorship to people interested in rapidly developing their psychic abilities. It is her mission to help spread the
light of psychic development to those who have an interest in
doing so. Learn more about how Tasha can help you develop your
spiritual gifts by visiting her at: www.tasharoubion.com

Manufactured by Amazon.ca
Bolton, ON

17805210R00083